THE ROYAL HORTICULTURAL SOCIETY
PRACTICAL GUIDES

FUCHSIAS

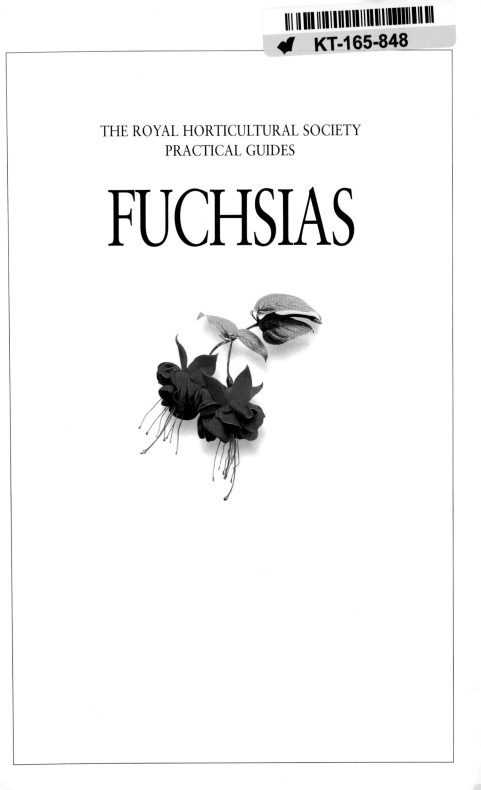

THE ROYAL HORTICULTURAL SOCIETY
PRACTICAL GUIDES

FUCHSIAS

GEORGE BARTLETT

DORLING KINDERSLEY

LONDON • NEW YORK • SYDNEY

www.dk.com

LONDON, NEW YORK, MUNICH,
MELBOURNE, DELHI

PROJECT EDITOR Simon Maughan

SERIES EDITOR Gillian Roberts
SERIES ART EDITOR Stephen Josland

SENIOR MANAGING EDITOR Mary-Clare Jerram
SENIOR MANAGING ART EDITOR Lee Griffiths

DTP DESIGNER Louise Paddick

PRODUCTION Mandy Inness

First published in Great Britain in 2000
Reprinted 2002
by Dorling Kindersley Limited,
80 Strand, London WC2R 0RL

A Penguin Company

A CIP catalogue record for this book is available from the British Library.
ISBN 0 7513 47183

Reproduced by Colourscan, Singapore
Printed and bound by Star Standard Industries, Singapore

See our complete catalogue at
www.dk.com

CONTENTS

GETTING TO KNOW FUCHSIAS 7

An introduction to fuchsias and the many ways in which they can be grown in the garden; bush, trailing, and standard fuchsias; flower forms and colours; foliage; and plants that harmonize with fuchsias.

CARING FOR YOUR FUCHSIAS 27

THE FUCHSIA GALLERY 55

A photographic guide to all kinds of fuchsias.

GETTING TO KNOW FUCHSIAS

WHAT ARE FUCHSIAS?

WITH THE SIMPLICITY of their pendulous flowers and the ease with which they can be grown, fuchsias are extremely popular plants. They are also truly versatile, from low creepers suitable for the rockery, through to fuchsias that can be trained and clipped to any shape imaginable. In milder climates, which are favoured by fuchsias, some will grow as large hedges or small trees.

A BRIEF HISTORY OF FUCHSIAS

The majority of wild fuchsias are found in the lower wooded foothills of Central and South America, and they became known to the modern world only in 1703, when *Fuchsia triphylla flore coccinea* was discovered by Father Charles Plumier. The name *Fuchsia* was given to honour the German botanist, Leonard Fuchs. The first plants were grown in Europe in the early 1790s, but hybridization did not begin until 1825; it is from those very early crosses that we have such a wealth of colour and form available to us today. Considerable progress continues to be made, and some of the results have been magnificent.

FUCHSIAS GIVE FAST RESULTS

Perhaps one of the most satisfying aspects of fuchsias is their speedy growth. Young plants purchased or rooted in early spring will effortlessly develop into flowering plants by early summer. Fuchsias that permanently reside in garden borders will grow tall new flowering stems from their root systems within just a few months.

◀ HANGING BLOOM
Fuchsias are famous for their pendulous flowers. These blooms belong to a bush fuchsia called 'Lye's Unique', which continues to be very popular, even though it was introduced over one hundred years ago.

◀ IN FULL GLORY *'Blush of Dawn' is a fully double fuchsia suitable for a hanging container.*

TYPES OF FUCHSIA

As soon as horticulturists were able to grow fuchsias successfully, hybridization began in earnest. Lovely new cultivars became available, and today we have fuchsias for most parts of the garden, all with their unmistakable and colourful flowers. Bush fuchsias, trailing fuchsias, and fuchsias grown as standards are the main categories of interest, but the diversity is great, so it is worth taking a deeper look.

WHAT ARE SPECIES FUCHSIAS?

Fuchsias that grow wild in their native habitats are known as Species fuchsias. Most of this group have reddish flowers

> Species fuchsias are the ancestors of all the modern cultivars

with long thin tubes and trumpet-shaped sepals and petals. There is a reason for this shape and colour; they attract humming-birds, which pollinate the flowers.

▲ *F. PANICULATA*
Known as "the lilac fuchsia" for its large bunches of very small flowers, this plant has very strong, upright growth, which makes it easy to grow – a good choice for a beginner.

▲ *F. MICROPHYLLA*
Like other Encliandra fuchsias (see facing page), this one has beautiful small flowers. It also has fern-like and delicate foliage.

▲ 'LOXENSIS'
Although given a cultivar name, this fuchsia is a hybrid between two Species fuchsias. It has upright and bushy, rampant growth.

F. PROCUMBENS
This is a popular
and easy fuchsia to
grow in a rock garden
or hanging container.
The trailing growth
is very attractive.

SPECIES FUCHSIAS TO GROW

There are more than one hundred Species fuchsias so far identified, although only a handful of these are available to gardeners. Specialist fuchsia nurseries are the best places to seek them out.

F. magellanica is without doubt the most popular Species fuchsia in cultivation. A considerable number of variants exist, and *F. magellanica* 'Versicolor', with its white and silvery pink leaf markings, is among the best. They are all very easy to grow and reliably frost hardy.

F. procumbens merits special attention as its upward-looking flowers make it unique. They are like miniature golden goblets with green sepals and blue pollen – colours very rarely found in fuchsias. The fruit, when they form, should be left on the plant as they are also attractive, being much larger than the small flowers.

ENCLIANDRA FUCHSIAS

A collection of fuchsias belonging to the Encliandra group will provide considerable interest. They are characterized by their small foliage and flowers, and long wiry stems, which are easily twined around wire shapes to produce interesting structures (*see pp.44–47*). *F. microphylla* subsp. *hidalgensis*, with white flowers, is ideal for this kind of topiary work. Scent is very rare for fuchsias, but a delicate perfume can be found in the extraordinary flowers of 'Neopolitan', which are white, maturing to red through pink; all three colours may be present at once.

RECOMMENDED SPECIES FUCHSIAS

F. arborescens Bunches of lilac-blue flowers.
F. boliviana Rose-red flowers with long, slender tubes and backward-curving sepals.
F. denticulata Long-tubed, dark red flowers with bright orange petals. Easy to grow.
F. fulgens Long, trumpet-shaped orange flowers. Several varieties.
F. glazioviana Small flowers with red sepals and violet petals. A strong and easy grower.
F. magellanica Many varieties exist in cultivation, all with variations in flower and foliage colour. Very frost hardy and easy to grow.
F. microphylla subsp. *hidalgensis* White flowers on wiry, spreading growth.
F. paniculata Lilac flowers and laurel-like foliage. Its vigour makes it easy to grow.
F. procumbens Small, upward-looking flowers on a creeping plant. Good for a beginner.
F. venusta Long and thin, carmine-red flowers. Strong, spreading growth best in a large pot.

RECOGNIZING FUCHSIA FLOWER SHAPES

VARIETY AND DIVISIONS
*Fuchsia flowers are usually tubular and hanging. Single
flowers have four petals, semi-double flowers have between
five and seven, and fully double flowers have eight or more.
Triphyllas have long-tubed, single flowers, and those of
F. procumbens point upwards.*

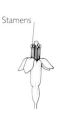

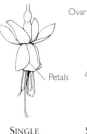

Stamens

Ovary

Sepals

Petals

Tube

Stigma

F. PROCUMBENS SINGLE SEMI-DOUBLE DOUBLE TRIPHYLLA TYPE

FUCHSIA FLOWER SHAPES

The legacy of over two centuries of fuchsia breeding gives the modern gardener a delightful array of flowers to choose from. Fuchsia flowers are almost always pendulous. They vary from very large to quite small, and they are borne more or less continuously through summer and autumn. Three main divisions exist –

single, semi-double and double – which are based on the number of petals a flower has. The annotated diagrams above show the anatomy of typical fuchsia flowers.

The fuchsia cultivars known as Triphyllas have long-tubed flowers with trumpet-shaped sepals and petals, and it is this distinctive characteristic that sets them apart from the rest.

▲ 'CITATION'
*The backward-curving sepals
on these single flowers expose
the four white petals.*

▲ 'PIPPA'
*This semi-double cultivar has
bright flowers with between
five and seven petals.*

▲ 'DARK EYES'
*The numerous petals of this
double-flowered bush fuchsia
are tightly rolled at the centre.*

VERSATILE GROWTH

- The vigorous growth of fuchsias is easily trained into different shapes (see pp.44–47).
- A standard fuchsia is really a trailing or a bush cultivar made to grow with a very long, bare stem, which branches only at the top.

BUSH AND TRAILING FUCHSIAS

When you read a description of a fuchsia in a nursery catalogue, the plant will usually be described as either a bush or a trailer.

The growth of bush fuchsias is further divided into upright or lax. Without doubt, the strong, upright growers will make the best bush fuchsias with little effort on your part. Those with lax growth, such as 'Swingtime', are best in hanging baskets or containers, although the growth is perhaps a little too stiff to trail naturally.

Trailing fuchsias have very lax growth, which naturally cascades over the edge of containers or walls, with flowers borne at the ends of the trails. Properly raised, they give a lot of colour. The finest standards are produced from trailing fuchsias, although bush types with strong, upright growth may be easier for the beginner.

▲ *F. MAGELLANICA*
The strong, upright growth of this bush fuchsia makes it suitable for use in a border. As it is frost hardy, it can be left outside and clipped as a hedge.

▲ 'CORALLINA'
The rather lax, spreading growth of this bush looks good trailing over a wall.

◄ 'TOM THUMB'
Classed as an upright bush, this small cultivar grows to only about 30cm (12in) tall.

THE COLOUR RANGE

THE DELICATE APPEARANCE of the fuchsia flower is enhanced by the attractive colour combinations produced by the tube, sepals, and petals. Virtually all colours of the spectrum are available, with the exception of pure yellow and true blue, from the purest of whites right through to very dark purple or near black. Perhaps the most popular fuchsias are those with delicate pastel shading.

MULTI-COLOURED FLOWERS

It must be the stark contrast or delicate variation between the colours of the sepals and petals that gives fuchsias their greatest appeal. Some double-flowered cultivars even show colour contrast between the petals, which gives rise to well-chosen names such as 'Peppermint Stick', although a simple description hardly does full justice to this large-flowered fuchsia with striped tubes and multi-coloured petals. The bold shading of 'Joy Patmore', with its pure waxy white sepals and rich carmine-pink petals, also demands attention. Another extremely striking colour combination is seen in 'Celia Smedley', whose pale rose-pink tube and sepals serve to enhance the vivid redcurrant colouring of the petals.

THE FUCHSIA SPECTRUM
With over 8,000 different fuchsias in cultivation, small wonder that there are colours to suit all tastes and moods. The enormous variation is incredible, from simple whites to frivolous pinks, and bright reds to sombre purples. It is often the particular size or shape of a flower, or the way in which it is carried, that can give a particular bloom its distinguishing features.

'SNOW WHITE'

'LEONORA'

'ANNABEL'

'ARABELLA'

'ALICE HOFFMAN'

SINGLE-COLOURED FLOWERS

Occasionally, all parts of the flower are exactly the same colour. Such flowers are usually referred to as "self-coloured", and there are many wonderful examples, like Turkey red 'Rufus', which has colouring so bright that it appears to glow. Most Triphylla fuchsias have flowers of just a single colour, and they are all very attractive, especially bright crimson 'Mary', which stands out like a beacon. A white Triphylla, 'Our Ted', has also been produced.

Many of the fuchsias with all-white flowers, however, tend to have less appeal as the white often takes on a slight greyish look with maturity, and they are easily bruised. Despite this, there is one white-flowered fuchsia that is far superior to any other; it is called 'Hawkshead' and is well worth seeking out.

If you are looking for the elusive yellow, try the unusual *F. procumbens*, which has that colour in small quantities. The realization of an all-yellow cultivar, however, continues to elude discovery.

TRADITIONAL FUCHSIA COLOURS

The colours that are still recognized as true fuchsia, the reds and the purples, are seen at their very best in some of the larger, double-flowered cultivars, like 'Royal Velvet'. Many have purple petals of the deepest hue, and in 'Gruss aus dem Bodethal', they verge on black. Even with this sombre colouring, the plants are extremely attractive.

'CORALLE'

'JACK SHAHAN'

'MARY'

'LA ROSITA'

'FEY'   'CECILE'

FUCHSIAS FOR FOLIAGE

ONE WOULD THINK that the great diversity of colour, shape, and size seen among fuchsia flowers would be riches enough; but there are also several fuchsias that produce delightful shades in the foliage, variegated or plain. Although these plants will (being fuchsias) continue to produce flowers as well, the beauty of foliage fuchsias sometimes comes into its own when both these elements combine.

THE RANGE OF FUCHSIA FOLIAGE

Quite a number of fuchsias are blessed with extremely attractive foliage; some have leaves that are golden green, while many others have variegated patterns enhanced with different colours and contrasting veins. Even some of the really frost hardy *F. magellanica* fuchsias display foliage colour variations. There are the golden yellow leaves of *F. magellanica* var. *gracilis* 'Aurea' and the distinctive cream, green, and pink variegation of *F. magellanica* var. *gracilis* 'Variegata', for example. When this group of fuchsias is allowed to grow in an open garden or as a hedge, the plants will produce both the delightful foliage and also an abundant supply of flowers.

As the colour of the foliage is visible even in young plants, choosing a fuchsia for its foliage when you are at a nursery is far easier than choosing for the flowers, since it is possible to see exactly what you are about to buy.

DISPLAYING THE FOLIAGE

Foliage plays a major role when it comes to the coordination of colour schemes. In the border, fuchsias of the Triphylla type, especially if grown as standards, add both height and colour to any display. Most Triphylla fuchsias have a delightful purple sheen on the undersides of the leaves, which will be subtly revealed in the slightest of breezes.

TRAILS OF COLOUR
The growth of 'Autumnale' is quite horizontal, which makes this plant an interesting choice for a hanging container. The young leaves start out green and yellow then age to dark red, salmon, and yellow.

◀ A FLORAL MATCH
*'Golden Marinka'
produces beautifully
variegated foliage as
well as an abundance
of flowers. It is a
trailing cultivar, and
it will quickly fill a
container with colour.*

▼ 'TOM WEST'
*The young leaves hold
the best colour, so
pinch out the growing
tips (see p.46).*

Within hanging containers, the bonus of coloured foliage cannot be over emphasized. It is possible to grow superb hanging containers filled entirely with a single fuchsia cultivar with remarkable foliage. 'Autumnale', with its stiff horizontal growth, can be used to create a fantastic

> Colourful foliage is a major component of modern planting schemes

parasol of autumn tints, which will win the admiration of any passer-by. As the best foliage colour is usually produced on the fresh young growth following the removal of the growing tips, the number of flowers actually produced on a fuchsia grown for its foliage can be relatively small.

FUCHSIAS WITH ATTRACTIVE FOLIAGE

'Autumnale' Golden and coppery red.
'Colne Greybeard' Silvery grey-green.
'Firecracker' Dark olive green with cream variegation. Fresh growth tinged with pink.
F. magellanica var. *molinae* **'Sharpitor'** Lovely cream and green variegation.
F. magellanica **'Versicolor'** Variegated and tinged with pink.

'Genii' Glowing golden yellow leaves. Best grown in full sun.
'Ornamental Pearl' Greenish cream, tinged pink.
'Rosecroft Beauty' Green and cream with cerise shading.
'Strawberry Delight' Pale green and red-bronze.
'Sunray' Creamy green suffused with cerise.
'Tropic Sunset' Green and reddish bronze.

PLANNING COMBINATIONS

WHETHER THEY ARE GROWN in the open garden, in patio tubs, or in hanging containers, fuchsias suit the company of other plants. The variety of such plants is legion and choices will depend entirely upon the likes and dislikes of each individual. Many people would agree that the best arrangement is to have fuchsias as the dominant plant with the others complementing them.

GOOD COLOUR COMBINATIONS

A great many fuchsia flowers have very strong colours; the bright reds, whites, and purples make it easy to plan a display of contrasting colours, but it is more usual to tone them down by using plants with more subtle or complementary hues. Many plants other than fuchsias are suitable for this purpose. Bear in mind, however, that pretty colour combinations can be accomplished by using fuchsias entirely on their own; the strong reds and purples mix well with the pastel shades and the pure whites. Different fuchsia cultivars each have their own growth habits and optimum flowering times, which might cause the display to become slightly uneven. If this is unacceptable, plant groups of one cultivar together.

▲ COLOUR BALANCE
The red and white of 'Checkerboard' is complemented by pinks and whites in this summer border.

◄ A COLOURFUL FOIL
The green and white variegated leaves of F. magellanica *'Versicolor' contrast with the autumn foliage of* Berberis thunbergii.

AN ENTRANCING COMBINATION
The bright flowers of 'Gartenmeister Bonstedt' stand out here against an underplanting of Helichrysum petiolare. *White or pastel-coloured fuchsias can be similarly enhanced if they are planted with strong-coloured flowers, such as purple-flowered verbenas.*

COMBINATIONS FOR CONTAINERS

For patio containers, height is often needed to give a display greater prominence. A fuchsia trained as a standard is one way to achieve this, although upright bedding plants, such as pelargoniums, begonias, or marigolds, with their striking colours, also work well. These could even be planted around the base of a standard. The sharpness of the edges of containers can be softened by allowing cascading plants to flow over the edges; try lobelias, which are available in a range of colours.

Lobelias are also excellent in hanging containers; the blue-flowered *Lobelia richardsonii* looks splendid with red and white fuchsias. *Glechoma hederacea* 'Variegata', which has long, trailing stems and scented leaves, is another favourite companion of fuchsias for hanging containers; it will cascade straight downward and give the impression of great depth. Consider also verbenas with their bright flowers and weaving stems, *Bidens ferulifolia* to introduce a bit of that elusive

Strong colours are set off by pastel shades, whites, and silvers

yellow into the display, and any of the trailing foliage plants, such as the silver *Helichrysum petiolare* or the variegated ivies. Remember that some fuchsias, as in 'Autumnale', have attractive leaves, and these can be intermingled into your display.

FUCHSIAS FOR THE OPEN GARDEN

FUCHSIAS ARE UNDOUBTEDLY at their best when they grow in the open garden. Planted permanently in beds made up completely of fuchsias or with other perennial plants, they will repay a thousandfold the minimal effort required. Although virtually any fuchsia will safely come through the winter if given proper winter protection (*see p.39*), it is the speed of production of the strong flowering branches that is of greatest importance. Fuchsias in the open garden are of little value if production of flowers is delayed until the autumn.

WHICH FUCHSIAS ARE HARDY?

A great many fuchsias are considered to be winter hardy in that they can remain in the open garden throughout winter, even when the temperature falls below freezing. *F. magellanica* and its variants are the hardiest of all the fuchsias, and there is, fortunately, considerable choice in their flowers and foliage. In a severe winter, it is possible that frost will kill the top growth, although new growth will emerge from the root system in the spring to form a new plant for that year. There are other strong and upright cultivars that are hardy: 'Phyllis' and 'Margaret' are just two.

SEA SPRAY AND POLLUTION

Gardeners often ask whether fuchsias are tolerant of traffic pollution or the effects of salt spray in coastal gardens. Although it is true that some – perhaps the tender and pastel-shaded flowers – may be affected, most fuchsias seem to be quite happy living alongside a busy road or beside the sea. Most gardeners rapidly learn by trial and error which plants are badly affected by adverse conditions.

▼ HERBACEOUS BORDER COMPANIONS
Interplanted with shrubs of a similar height, hardy fuchsias can be a permanent feature.

◀ FUCHSIA HEDGE
In milder areas, it is possible to use hardy fuchsias as hedges. Plants grown close together give extra protection to one another, so the top growth is more likely to survive where winters are frosty.

▼ IN THE WOODS
Like other types of F. magellanica, *white-flowered* F. magellanica *'Alba' is very frost hardy.*

HARDY FUCHSIAS IN BORDERS

Any garden border is enlivened by the addition of hardy fuchsias, with their enduring flower displays. Mass plantings of one cultivar can make a bold statement, but it is more common for them to be used as part of a mixed border with other shrubs, trees, and herbaceous perennials.

Bush fuchsias lend height and colour to a mixed border and are usually planted near the middle; smaller annuals and perennials are placed near the front, and trees and taller shrubs go behind where they may provide light shade, which fuchsias love.

Hardy fuchsias grown as standards, placed strategically around the border, can compensate for any lack of height. It is imperative, however, that standards are removed from the border and given protection before the onset of frosts. Even if the standards are considered very hardy, frost will kill the stem.

FUCHSIAS IN RAISED BEDS

The beauty of fuchsias is often seen to best effect when they are grown in raised beds. Trailing forms are particularly useful in this situation as the dangling stems relieve the starkness of the wall edges. Bush fuchsias will add height to the display.

FUCHSIAS FOR SUMMER BEDDING

THERE ARE SOME FUCHSIAS that are not sufficiently hardy to endure a frosty winter if left outside. In such cases, these fuchsias can simply be treated in the same way as other half-hardy plants and given temporary protection during the cold months (*see p.39*). When the warm weather returns in spring, the fuchsias can be planted out in the open garden again.

COLOUR AND HEIGHT

Fuchsias in summer bedding displays allow for considerable scope when it comes to colour schemes, especially if they are co-ordinated with other plants (*see pp.16–17*). The inclusion of bush and standard fuchsias, perhaps of the more unusual cultivars such as the Triphyllas, brings height into the display, which is an all-important ingredient that bedding schemes often lack. Not only does this present a very attractive display, but the fuchsias will also act as perfect foils for lower-growing bedding plants, like begonias or busy Lizzies. A border edged with lobelias and alyssum serves to lead the eye inwards to the colouring of the fuchsias.

HOW TO GROUP YOUR FUCHSIAS

Eye-catching displays are almost always the result of careful planning, and it pays to follow some key principles. The most fundamental of these is to position taller specimens at the back of the border to create a backdrop, which will emphasize those plants at the centre of the display.

▲ OUT IN THE SUN
Unlike most fuchsias, those that belong to the Triphylla group tolerate full sun as well as partial shade.

▶ AN EXOTIC AURA
Any summer garden that has a blossoming border display full of fuchsias will have an unmistakably exotic atmosphere.

Further impact is made if fuchsias of the same cultivar are grouped together, preferably in threes or fives. You can make a formal bedding display even more striking by dotting standard fuchsias around the border, but bear in mind that they need the support of strong stakes to prevent damage by gusts of wind.

LET THE ROOTS SPREAD OUT

There is always some debate as to whether or not fuchsias for summer bedding should be left in their pots when they are planted out. Removing the pots gives the roots plenty of room to develop and seek food and moisture, which results in larger flowering plants. The only problem comes when the plants need to be lifted in the autumn (*see p.39*), but the benefits of bigger plants with less anxiety over watering and feeding will more than compensate for this slight inconvenience.

▲ BOLD COLOURS
'Leverkusen', a bush Triphylla fuchsia, has intense flowers, which contrast well with other bright colours.

◀ ADDED HEIGHT
The combination of bush and standard fuchsias in a summer border brings height into the display – an important ingredient for successful design.

FUCHSIAS FOR CONTAINERS

No MATTER HOW LARGE or small a garden you may have, or even if you have no garden at all, it is always possible to enjoy growing fuchsias in containers. Fuchsias are perhaps the perfect plant for this type of display, and a visit to any garden centre will open your eyes to the great choice of containers available. Let your imagination wander; old and unusual receptacles, like chimney pots or wheelbarrows, can all be used as containers to make attractive features.

THE USEFULNESS OF CONTAINERS

Perhaps the most useful feature of growing plants in containers is the flexibility. The positions of containers can be changed to present a different perspective, and when the winter sets in, fuchsias are easily moved to shelter, if necessary.

Pots arranged on tiered staging can make a very decorative display, particularly when the plants are in full flower – all summer long for fuchsias. Ensure that containers are stable in windy conditions, however, as it would be a shame to see a well-grown plant rolling around on the ground with a smashed pot. Wrought iron stands that hold six or more containers are stable and attractive, and simple displays of grouped pots dotted around on the patio are also appealing. Do not worry too much about the look of the pot – after all, it is not the pot that will eventually catch the eye but the cascading and beautiful effect of the plants within it.

A STANDARD AS A FOCAL POINT
For a point of focus on a patio, pot up a single standard fuchsia, and underplant it with complementary flowers or foliage.

CONTAINER CULTIVARS

'Annabel' White flowers flushed with pink.
'Auntie Jinks' White and purple flowers.
'Blush of Dawn' White and pink flowers.
'Cascade' Pale pink and rich scarlet flowers.
'Dark Eyes' Red and violet-blue flowers.
'Eternal Flame' Salmon-pink and pink flowers.
'Glowing Embers' Pink and red flowers.
'Hula Girl' Deep rose-pink and white flowers.
'Kimberly' Pink and deep blue flowers.
'La Campanella' White and purple flowers.
'Marinka' Excellent red-flowered cultivar.
'Postiljon' White and rose-purple flowers.
'Quasar' White and rich violet flowers.
'Rosebud' White and rose-pink flowers.
'Salmon Cascade' Pink and orange-red flowers.
'Swingtime' Scarlet and pure white flowers.
'White Galore' White, fully double flowers.

STANDARD FUCHSIAS IN POTS

Patios and other paved areas can benefit greatly from one or more standard fuchsias in pots, to relieve an appearance of flatness, and to gain height and visual interest. In its simplest form, one standard fuchsia is planted at the centre of a container and surrounded at the base with either lower-growing or trailing fuchsias, or with other types of plants (*see pp.30–31*). Those specimens used to complement a standard fuchsia depend entirely on personal choice, but consideration should be given to the harmonizing of the colours (*see pp.16–17*).

Standard fuchsias are really quite easy to grow from a rooted cutting (*see p.47*). They do not require any special expertise; a standard fuchsia is in fact simply a bush or trailing fuchsia that has been made to branch on the top of a tall stem, which you will first have to grow. If you prefer not to grow one yourself, many garden centres sell ready-trained standards, although they may be relatively expensive. A standard fuchsia, with a clear stem between 45–75cm (18–30in) tall, will probably serve you best. Always make sure that it is well supported with a strong, secure stake.

▲ OPPORTUNITY FOR COLOUR
The bright blue flowers of Felicia amelloides *contrast perfectly with 'Checkerboard', which is grown here as a standard.*

▼ A MOVABLE FEAST FOR THE EYES
Pot-grown fuchsias love a tranquil spot in the shade of a small tree during summer.

FUCHSIAS FOR HANGING BASKETS

It is not necessary for hanging baskets to be made of wire mesh; any receptacle that can hold potting compost and has drainage holes will be satisfactory. Wooden containers, made to any shape or size you require, can be suspended from brackets so that your plants trail downward in an eye-catching display. Always consider carefully how containers are to be suspended; all brackets used should be securely fixed on the wall and of sufficient length and strength to support the full weight of the container when it is completely planted up.

FUCHSIAS FOR WINDOWBOXES

Windowboxes can be used to great effect to display a colourful selection of fuchsias. Concentrate more on the lower-growing or smaller-flowered types, and allow the cascading stems of trailing fuchsias to spill over the edge. Try some of the dwarf fuchsia cultivars, like these members of the 'Thumb' family: 'Tom Thumb' has red and purple flowers, those of 'Lady Thumb' are red and white, and those of 'Son of Thumb' are red and lilac. As each of these

▲ BUNDLES OF BLOOM
Do not worry too much about the look of the container – these fuchsias and petunias have completely enveloped their hanging basket in a bundle of bloom.

▼ FUCHSIAS WITH FUCHSIAS
Here, bush fuchsia 'Tom Woods' is under-planted with 'Jack Shahan', a trailing cultivar.

◀ WINDOW DISPLAY
*Concentrate on
lower-growing or
trailing plants for
windowboxes so that
they do not prevent
light from reaching
indoors.*

▼ A MIXED POT
*In this terracotta pot,
the upright and bushy
growth of 'Preston
Guild' mingles with
argyranthemums and
silvery* Helichrysum
petiolare.

plants grows only to a bushy height of
about 23cm (9in), they will not prevent
any light from passing through windows.
They all look good together.

FUCHSIAS FOR INDOOR DISPLAY

Fuchsias make extraordinarily fine indoor
table decorations, although they are not
really house plants as they require a

> For short spells only,
> fuchsias in containers
> make fine indoor displays

humidity in the atmosphere that is not
usually present indoors. It is possible,
however, to use fuchsias as temporary
visitors to the home if they are placed
in pots on a tray of permanently moist
pebbles, which will keep the air humid.

Fuchsias that have been raised as cuttings
on the windowsill, and have known no
conditions other than the dryness of a
house, may give quite satisfactory long-
term displays with minimum effort.

CARING FOR YOUR FUCHSIAS

CHOOSING AND BUYING FUCHSIAS

THE BEST TIME to buy young fuchsias for summer colour is in early spring. Plants should be available from your local garden centre, and specialist fuchsia nurseries will be able to help with less common ones. The plants on sale will have been raised as cuttings the previous autumn and should be growing strongly. Examine each plant to make sure that there are no signs of any pests or diseases; look in particular at the stem and lower branches to check for any signs of mould.

SELECTING THE BEST PLANTS

Unless you intend to grow a standard fuchsia, choose a well-branched plant – one with the branches growing quite closely together. These fuchsias will produce the greatest density of flowers. If you see any young fuchsia plants in the nursery with tall, upright growth and plenty of distance between the leaf nodes, then these will be the easiest to train as standards.

BUYING TIPS
• Have a firm idea of how many plants you want to buy. It is easy to get carried away.
• If you intend to grow a standard, ensure the young plant has a strong, straight stem.
• Plants must be labelled "frost hardy" if for year-round outdoor display in frosty areas.
• Select trailing cultivars for hanging baskets.

Closely branched growth produces the best flowers

Tall growth is easier to train into a standard

Flowers borne in leaf axils

Small fuchsias in trays are easy to transport

Clear label helps you choose the right type of fuchsia

WHAT TO BUY
Fuchsias are available to buy at different stages of development. Smaller plants are obviously easier to carry, although an older plant that has been trained to shape for you will save you the trouble at home. Also check the label to ensure that the fuchsia you intend to buy is suitable for its future role.

◄ *F. MAGELLANICA* VAR. *GRACILIS Slim flowers are carried on strong, wiry growth.*

PLANTING OUT IN THE GARDEN

WELL-DRAINED SOIL and bright light to dappled shade from the sun are the main requirements of almost all cultivated fuchsias. The soil should be thoroughly prepared before planting, and a site that is in shade during the hottest part of the day is ideal. Plant your young fuchsias, which should be growing strongly in their pots, only when all risk of frost has passed. Give any Species fuchsias as much uninterrupted root room as possible.

SOIL PREPARATION

It is important to prepare the ground thoroughly before you plant, as this is the way to get the best out of your fuchsias. First, clear the soil of persistent weeds by hand or with a suitable herbicide, then dig the soil over to the depth of one spade blade, forking in plenty of well-rotted organic matter as you go (*below*). Finally, rake over the surface to break up any remaining clods of soil. In heavy, clay-like soil, incorporate copious quantities of grit or compost to open out the soil and improve aeration and drainage. Equally, light soil may need extra organic matter. Avoid digging when the ground is sodden, as you may damage the soil structure.

ENRICH THE SOIL WITH ORGANIC MATTER
Unless your soil is already very rich, digging in plenty of organic matter will improve the soil's drainage, aeration, fertility, and moisture-holding properties, particularly if it is light and sandy. To avoid back strain, keep your back straight when digging, and take a break as soon as you start to feel tired.

THE BEST SOIL ADDITIVES

COMPOST
The contribution of organic matter to the productivity of the garden is enormous. It is easy to prepare from your garden and kitchen waste, which must first be allowed to rot down well. Compost improves the soil structure, adds some nutrients, and encourages the beneficial activity of earthworms.

WELL-ROTTED ANIMAL MANURE
Preferably with a high straw content, this serves the same purpose as compost. Avoid fresh manure, which may be toxic to plants.

LEAFMOULD
A fibrous and flaky soil improver derived from decomposed leaves.

WATER-RETAINING GRANULES
These granules are especially useful in soil that is prone to drying out. They hold many times their weight in water and are commonly used in container plantings.

GRIT OR GRAVEL
Improves drainage on heavy clay or compacted soils.

PLANTING OUTSIDE FOR SUMMER BEDDING

In frost-prone areas, tender fuchsias may be grown in the garden in summer as seasonal plants. It is possible to plant them in the ground still in their pots, which certainly makes life easier when they are lifted in autumn. If you do remove the plants from their pots, however, you will be rewarded with bigger, more freely flowering fuchsias.

Leave a distance of about 45cm (18in) between the plants if individual specimens are being used, or a distance of about 23cm (9in) between the plants if you prefer groups of three or four. The beds will fill out more quickly with closer planting, but the plants may crowd each other; wider spacing will leave gaps for weeds.

1 Arrange the fuchsias into their display positions while they are still in their pots. Check the spacing (*above*), then water them well prior to planting.

2 Dig a hole for each plant, large enough to hold its pot. Place the plant in the hole, with or without its pot, and firm the soil. Add more soil to cover the root ball.

3 Water in well. Plants that have been left in their pots will need to be watered and fed individually throughout the summer, even if it has been raining (*see p.36*).

PLANTING FROST-HARDY FUCHSIAS

The best time to plant a hardy border is in spring, after all risk of frost has passed. Ensure that the soil is well prepared (*see facing page*), and the fuchsias to be planted are healthy, with moist compost. Since each plant's root system needs to be protected from frost, deep planting is essential. Make a saucer-shaped dip in the ground to a depth of 8cm (3in). In the centre of the dip, dig a hole large enough to hold the plant's root ball, then place the plant in the hole so the top of the root ball is level with the bottom of the dip. Soil will naturally fill the dip over summer, and the plant will be at the correct depth in time for winter. Water regularly, and feed with a phosphate-rich fertilizer to encourage healthy roots.

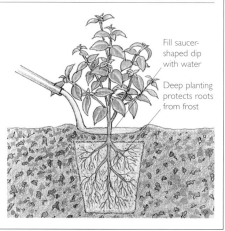

Fill saucer-shaped dip with water

Deep planting protects roots from frost

PLANTING FUCHSIAS IN CONTAINERS

FUCHSIAS IN CONTAINERS will give you a display throughout summer. Pots, windowboxes, and troughs are all ideal, although any sort of container can be used as long as it has drainage holes to prevent waterlogging. Raising the container slightly will also promote drainage. If the container will be in some sun, you could mix in some water-retaining granules; in larger containers, where there is more soil surface exposed, pebbles and gravel will help retain moisture.

YOU NEED:

TOOLS
• Trowel

MATERIALS
• Bucket
• Multi-purpose potting compost
• Horticultural grit
• Classic planter, box, or barrel
• Drainage crocks (or sacking, gravel, or polystyrene)

PLANTS USED
• 'Paula Jane' (standard) x 1
• 'Barbara Windsor' x 4

PLANTING A CONTAINER

1 **Any good quality** potting compost will do for fuchsias. Mix in grit to add weight, or the plants may topple in the wind.

2 **Place drainage crocks** at the base of the wooden planter, then fill the bottom with potting compost and gently firm it down.

3 **Remove the standard fuchsia** from its pot, and stand it on the compost in the planter. Gently tease out the roots, and ensure the stem is firmly staked up to the top.

4 **Position the pots** of the smaller fuchsias around the base of the standard. Assess how much space to allow, taking into account growing habit, such as trailing stems.

5 Use a trowel to completely fill the planter, around the empty pots in the top, with potting compost. Gently firm the compost, so that there are no air pockets, and fill in any gaps.

▼ THE COMPLETED PICTURE *'Paula Jane' is here trained as a standard, and used in this way it gives height and impact to the planting. Four plants of bushy 'Barbara Windsor' fill the corners.*

6 Remove the pots to leave a shape the exact size of the root ball of the smaller fuchsias, then drop these plants into their new holes. Fill with compost to just below the container edge. Water everything in well.

ADDITIONAL HINTS
• The use of a single fuchsia cultivar often works well in this kind of display.
• Add high-nitrogen fertilizer at the start of the season to boost foliage growth.
• Water-retaining granules mixed into the compost will help fuchsias in sunny sites.
• Frequent watering may leach out nutrients; restore with regular feeding (*see p.36*).

HANGING BASKETS

THE EARLIER IN THE SEASON that a basket can be filled, the better it will look. A basket made up in early spring will be well grown and ready for display as soon as summer begins. In cold areas, keep baskets in the greenhouse until all risk of frost has passed. A fully planted basket can be very heavy, so it is essential that any fixing from which a basket is hung is sufficiently secure. Also make sure that plants in the basket will not get damaged by being blown against a wall.

SINGLE AND MIXED PLANTINGS

Fuchsias look very effective in hanging baskets, and a more even display is made when plants of just one cultivar are grown together. A 35cm (14in) basket will hold five fuchsias from 9cm (3½in) pots: one in the centre and four around the edge. An upright cultivar at the centre will give extra height. The step-by-step guide on the following three pages shows how to plant a mixed basket; the procedure is the same for a single planting of fuchsias.

THE FINISHED BASKET
A rounded shape like this is one of the easiest to produce and maintain. Place the most upright-growing plant in the centre and surround it with trailing plants. Keeping to one cultivar ensures even flowering.

SUITABLE PLANTS

'**Annabel**' Easily trained, versatile trailer with double flowers, rose-flushed white.

'**Auntie Jinks**' Trailer; free-flowering over a long season. Purple, white, and pink-red blooms.

'**Autumnale**' Grown for its colourful young leaves. Scarlet flowers.

'**Cascade**' Excellent in a basket. White-flushed sepals and deep rose petals.

'**Frosted Flame**' Superb in a basket. Curling white sepals and flame red blooms.

'**Hidcote Beauty**' Creamy white sepals and pale pink petals. Free flowering.

'**Marinka**' Vigorous, free flowering. Dark red blooms.

'**Peter Crooks**' Triphylla fuchsia, with bright orange-red flowers in bunches at the ends of branches.

PLANTING A MIXED HANGING BASKET

To get the most from your mixed hanging basket, aim to create an envelope of loose and trailing stems that will camouflage the container. Set trailing plants into the side of the basket (*see p.34, step 4*) as well as in the top. Use only young, healthy plants, and to retain the potting compost and hold moisture, make sure the basket is properly lined. Various liners are available, such as coir fibre, foam, wool, and recycled paper.

YOU NEED:

TOOLS
• Bucket or large flowerpot
• Scissors or craft knife
• Plastic bowl or bucket

MATERIALS
• 35cm (14in) wire hanging basket
• Coir fibre liner
• Potting compost
• Slow-release fertilizer
• Water-retaining granules
• Polythene sheet

PLANTS USED
• Trailing lobelia × 2
• *Helichrysum petiolare* × 2
• Fuchsia × 2
• Ivy-leaved pelargonium × 2
• Trailing petunia × 2
• *Felicia amelloides* 'Variegata' × 1

LINING THE BASKET

1 **Place the basket** on a bucket or large flowerpot so that it is centred and level, to make it easier to fill and plant the basket. Fit the coir fibre liner, making several cuts, as shown, to ensure a snug fit.

2 **Press the coir** liner firmly against the bottom and sides of the basket, as it will be when filled with compost. Use scissors to trim off any liner that extends above the rim of the basket, to make a neat edge.

3 **Using a sharp** pair of scissors or a craft knife, make slits about 5cm (2in) long in the side of the liner for planting in tiers. Trailing plants inserted in slits at one or two levels below the surface of the basket will fill out and eventually conceal the wire frame.

PLANTING UP

1 **Empty the** potting compost into a plastic bowl or bucket and mix in slow-release fertilizer and water-retaining granules, according to the manufacturer's instructions.

2 **Add the prepared compost** to cover the bottom of the basket, filling up to the level of the first tier of slits cut in the side of the liner. Shake down the compost.

3 **To protect** the trailing plants that are to be inserted through the liner, wrap each in a piece of polythene sheet to form a cone over the stems and leaves. (It is normally not necessary to plant trailing fuchsias in tiers like this, as their stems will naturally cascade over the edge of the container.)

4 **Insert trailing** plants – in this case lobelia and *Helichrysum petiolare* – through the slits made in the liner. Working from the inside, thread each plant through, carefully keeping the polythene cone in position to protect the stems and leaves. When the plant is in position, with the root ball on the inside of the liner and the leaves and stems on the outside, gently unwrap and remove the polythene cone.

5 **Continue to plant** the bottom tier. Gently tease out the root balls and add potting compost, working it around the roots and filling to within 5cm (2in) of the rim.

6 **Plant trailing plants** – here, fuchsias, pelargoniums, and petunias – around the rim, spaced so that they are not immediately above the plants in the lower tiers.

7 **Add more compost,** working it around the roots and firming gently. Leave a gap in the centre for a bushy plant. *Felicia amelloides* 'Variegata', which is used in this planting, has blue daisy-like flowers and variegated cream-splashed leaves.

FINISHING THE BASKET
Complete planting by topping up with compost so that the surface is about 2.5cm (1in) below the rim of the basket. Water thoroughly. Keep the compost moist while the plants become established, but do not overwater.

ROUTINE CARE

FUCHSIAS ARE NORMALLY forest-dwelling plants, so they thrive in conditions where there is light, dappled shade and reasonably high humidity. The soil around fuchsias should be kept fertile and just moist, and since most are intolerant of hard frost, you will need to offer them some kind of winter protection if you live in an area where frost is likely.

FEEDING AND WATERING

During the growing season, feed fuchsias regularly with a balanced fertilizer; it will ensure strong growth and profuse flowering. Guidelines may suggest a weekly feed, but many experts prefer to feed each time they water, using a solution diluted to about a quarter of the recommended strength. Apply plain water once a week if this method is used, to wash the soil of excessive nutrients.

WATERING A POT
Water can be applied either in the top of a pot or from below, in a saucer, but do not let the pot stand permanently in water.

Promote healthy growth by regular feeding

Water applied at the soil surface will seep down to the roots

Drainage holes let water out and air in

TIPS ON FEEDING

• Slow-release fertilizer mixed into the potting compost lasts for one to three months; after this, it is necessary to use liquid feed.
• Allow a quarter of an hour for a potted fuchsia to soak up water from a saucer, then throw away any excess.
• Overfeeding will only damage fuchsias.
• Feed fuchsias grown for their attractive leaves with a high-nitrogen fertilizer.

RENEWING THE DISPLAY

Once the first flowers begin to appear in early summer, relax and enjoy the show; no more training or pinching out of the growing tips is needed. To maintain the quality of the bloom, however, regularly remove any flowers that are past their best; once berries begin to form, the flowering display may come to an early conclusion.

Many fuchsias with ornamental leaves produce their best colouring on very young growth, which can be encouraged by the continual pinching out of the growing tips. Any emergent shoots that have reverted back to their original all-green colouring must also be removed.

DEADHEADING
Regular removal of shrivelled or damaged flowers will prolong the display and maintain its perfection.

SUMMER SHADING

During periods of very hot weather, it is necessary to keep your fuchsias as cool as possible. In most climates, it will be sufficient to provide them with shade, but if they are growing under glass, it will be necessary either to move the plants outside or to provide special shading. An exception to the rule are Triphylla fuchsias, which seem to come into their own in full sun. Conversely, never put fuchsias in a position that is too dark.

HINTS ON SHADING

• Shade the glass in greenhouses either with blinds or shade paint, and regularly damp down the floors and staging.
• Aim to keep the temperature below 27°C (81°F), since many fuchsias tend to stop growing and flowering above this point.
• Positions not facing the midday sun are good, as are sites half-shaded by taller plants.
• Black pots are death traps in full sun.

◄ SHADING IN THE GREENHOUSE
If you grow fuchsias in a greenhouse, they must be kept as cool as possible by shading the glass. Circulating fans will help to maintain an evenly low temperature.

► SHADING IN THE GARDEN
Partial shade is not only good for fuchsias, but it also suits a great many herbaceous perennials, so mixed plantings need not suffer. Make sure that any shaded area chosen for the display of fuchsias can easily be seen from the house or garden, and thin out old trees and shrubs if the shade created by them is too dense; heavy shade will seriously restrict growth.

REPOTTING A MATURE FUCHSIA

As a fuchsia begins to outgrow its pot, it will lose its vigour and start to show signs of poor health, such as yellowing leaves. When this happens, the time has come to repot it into a new container. Select a pot one size larger; go up in size by about 2.5cm (1in) each time to keep the plant in scale with the size of the pot. If a container of a similar size is chosen, then it may be necessary to trim the roots back a little. Make sure that the new pot is clean to avoid introducing pests or diseases.

1 **Check the** potting compost to determine whether it is necessary to repot. Compacted compost will no longer be free-draining or permeable to the air. Moss on the surface is a sure sign of sour soil.

2 **Ease the plant** gently from its pot and begin to crumble some of the soil away from the crowded roots.

3 **Free up** and tease out the roots. If the new pot is the same size as the old pot, it is advisable to cut back thick and gnarled roots by about one-third. Leave the thin fibrous roots intact.

4 **Put fresh compost** in the new pot, lower in the plant, then add more compost around the edges and firm in. For standards, tie in a new support stake. Water well.

5 **Trim back** the old top growth to encourage new flowering shoots. A severe pruning, leaving just one-third of the top growth, will revitalize an old plant.

OVERWINTERING INDOORS AND OUT

Potted fuchsias will come safely through a cold winter if two simple rules are obeyed: the plants should be kept frost free, and the root system should not be allowed to dry out. For frost-tender fuchsias, the protection of a garage or shed is adequate, especially if the pots are placed in a large, insulated box. Fuchsias survive a few dark months in a box, but trim the shoots back when the plants are brought out in spring. Hardy fuchsias remain outdoors; a thick layer of mulch spread around the roots will give extra protection.

TIPS ON OVERWINTERING

• After the first severe frost, do not remove the dead branches from hardy fuchsias. These branches will protect the root system.

• Check regularly to ensure the soil around potted fuchsias is not allowed to dry out.

• If fuchsias are to keep growing, site them in a well-lit greenhouse at 5–7°C (41–45°F).

• If you are unsure about the hardiness of any fuchsias left outdoors, then take cuttings in autumn and overwinter these indoors.

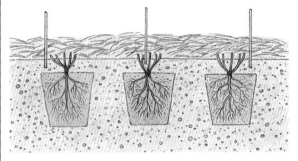

BURYING TENDER FUCHSIAS
This is a useful method where there is no room indoors for overwintering. Dig a hole or trench deep enough to take the whole root ball and some of the stem. Fill the hole with garden soil, cover with straw, and mark the site. This method does not work for all fuchsias, so it may be wise to take cuttings too.

PROMOTING SPRING GROWTH

Fuchsias flower only on the current season's new growth, so you need to encourage fresh growth by severe pruning. As the temperature rises in spring, new shoots will appear. If the winter has been very mild, shoots may appear from the old branches. It is important, however, to cut back most of the old wood, even if it is bearing shoots, in order to encourage strong fresh growth from ground level upward. Apply fertilizer to boost growth and encourage the regeneration of the plants.

PRUNING A STANDARD FUCHSIA
After a cold winter in an unheated greenhouse, the top growth has died back. Cut back old wood and allow the new growth to develop.

PRUNING A HARDY BUSH FUCHSIA
Leave the old growth until spring, then cut the old branches back to near ground level, even if new shoots are emerging higher up.

HOW TO PROPAGATE FUCHSIAS

GENERALLY, THERE ARE three types of propagation: seed, cuttings, and grafting. Grafting is little practised, and seeds from cultivars are rarely as good as the parent plants, but a fuchsia cutting – a small piece of cut stem – will, when rooted, produce a plant that carries foliage and flowers identical to the plant from which it is taken. Even the least green-fingered of gardeners can root fuchsia cuttings successfully; the only requirements are moisture and warmth.

TAKING CUTTINGS

In spring or late autumn, there is always a plentiful supply of potential cuttings on a fuchsia. First, choose a healthy, vigorous plant, then simply remove a section of stem. On the whole, it is best to use a sharp knife (it provides a clean cut), but your finger and thumb will do even though this may cause bruising. A single stem can yield quite a number of cuttings if the three techniques shown below are combined.

TAKING A SOFT-TIP CUTTING
This is the easiest cutting to root. Sever the tip of a young branch just above the next set of leaves down the stem.

AN INTERNODAL CUTTING
Remove the soft tip, then cut just above the second set of leaves to give a pair of leaves between two pieces of stem.

A SINGLE-LEAF CUTTING
Cut the stem as for an internodal cutting. The cutting will then need to be sliced in half (below).

A SOFT-TIP CUTTING
This cutting consists of a growing tip, an immature set of leaves, and a mature set.

TRIM THE LEAVES
With this internodal cutting, the leaves can be reduced in size to lessen water loss.

SLICING A SINGLE-LEAF CUTTING
Carefully slice along the stem between the leaves to make two single-leaf cuttings, each with a shoot growing in the leaf axil. Once planted, the shoot will grow into a new plant.

ROOTING CUTTINGS IN CUTTING COMPOST

Fuchsia cuttings will root in almost any substance that retains moisture, including pure water, although the ideal cutting compost seems to be an equal mixture of peat and vermiculite. This is an open and loose, low-nutrient medium, which allows for the development of a healthy root system. With the use of a propagator to keep conditions warm and moist, your cuttings can be left to their own devices and will root in about two to three weeks.

PRACTICAL HINTS

• Any transparent container that can be sealed, such as a jam jar or cut-down lemonade bottle, will serve as a propagator.
• Do not firm the cutting compost – let it remain open and loose.
• Sharp sand is an alternative to vermiculite.
• Take care with heated propagators as excessive warmth will kill the roots.
• Do not allow leaves of cuttings to overlap.

1 Make a small hole, then push the cuttings gently into the compost so that the leaves are just above the surface. If you are unsure about ease of rooting, begin by dipping the base of each stem in hormone rooting powder or liquid.

2 Continue to place the cuttings until all the cells in the strip have been filled. Instead of a modular tray, like the one shown on this page, you can fill a single pot with several cuttings.

3 Water the cuttings using a watering can fitted with a fine rose, then place them in a sealed propagator. Choose a cool position – about 16°C (61°F) should be sufficient – with shade from direct sun. No further action needs to be taken until new growth appears.

ROOTING CUTTINGS IN FLORISTS' FOAM

This method of propagation is a very simple way to root soft-tip cuttings. Florists' foam is used instead of cutting compost, which makes it a tidy job: something that can be done in the kitchen. The soft-tip cuttings are prepared in the normal way (*see p.40*) and allowed to root in the warm and humid atmosphere of a propagator. Only when they have rooted are they transferred to pots – still with the foam attached – where the plants will continue to grow.

PRACTICAL HINTS

• Take care not to crush the stems of the cuttings when handling. It is best to handle cuttings by their leaves.

• Fuchsia cuttings are susceptible to a range of pests and diseases, so take cuttings only from clean and healthy plants.

• When potting up, cover all the foam with potting compost. Exposed foam acts as a wick and draws moisture away from the roots.

1 **Cut a block** of florists' foam into 2.5cm (1in) cubes. Soak the cubes in water for 10–15 minutes, then place them in a saucer or tray. Use a knitting needle to make a 1cm (½in) deep hole in the centre of each cube.

2 **Insert a cutting** into each cube. Cuttings should sit with the leaves just above the surface and the base touching the bottom of the hole. If the hole is too shallow, deepen it with the needle; do not push the cutting.

3 **Add water** to the saucer to a depth of about 1cm (½in). Label and place the cuttings in a sealed propagator, or in a plastic bag (tented with stakes), in bright indirect light at about 16°C (61°F), until rooted (*inset*).

4 **Pot up the cuttings** singly into 8cm (3in) pots of potting compost when their roots show through the foam. Cover the foam with 5mm (¼in) of compost to prevent the roots from drying out.

POTTING UP

Once the cuttings start to show healthy top growth, a root system has begun to form. This growth will develop into a strong, bushy fuchsia only if the rooted cuttings are moved to larger containers.

For the first few days, remove the lid of the propagator during daylight hours to accustom the rooted cuttings to a less humid atmosphere. Finally, remove the lid altogether, then pot each cutting into its own 8cm (3in) container. Place a small quantity of fresh potting compost (*see below*) in the base of the new pot, position the young plant inside with its roots spread out, and fill around the roots with more compost. Gently tap the filled pot on the bench to settle the compost. Do not firm by hand; subsequent waterings do this job naturally.

As the young plant continues to grow, it may be necessary to pot it on several times. To minimize root disturbance, use the technique shown on pp.30–31, steps 4–6, to mould shapes into fresh compost into which the root ball can be lifted.

POTTING ON
If left in a confined root space for too long, growth will slow down and may even stop. Giving fuchsias additional space for the roots to develop is therefore an essential part of cultivation; the usual advice is to pot on cuttings into pots approximately 2.5cm (1in) larger.

WHICH POTTING COMPOST TO USE

When faced with the considerable amount of choice available today, it is no wonder that newcomers get worried about which potting compost to use. In fact, there is no need to worry as fuchsias will grow well in virtually any type of potting compost, so long as it is moist but well drained (not wet) and well aerated. Avoid the temptation to use soil from the garden; it often gives disappointing results. Some potting composts are improved by certain additives; you might find it useful, for example, to add water-retaining granules to the compost if the container is to be positioned in full sun. As for nutrients, the amount contained in a compost when it is purchased is of little importance, since fuchsias are fed from a relatively early age during watering (*see p.36*).

SOIL-BASED POTTING COMPOSTS

These composts provide ideal conditions for long-term growth. They are rich in organic matter, free draining, and their good structure ensures adequate aeration of the roots.

PEAT OR PEAT SUBSTITUTES

Although these soilless composts dry out more quickly than soil-based ones and are prone to waterlogging, peat or peat substitutes may be improved by the addition of grit (to give added weight and stability), and perlite or vermiculite (to improve drainage, provide aeration to the roots, and remoisten dry compost). The quantity of these products to be added is not critical and can be based on the premise that if it feels right, then it probably is.

TRAINING INTO SHAPES

T HE TRAINING OR SHAPING of a fuchsia can begin once the young cutting has developed a good root system; in fact, as soon as it is transferred into its first individual pot. For most, the same basic type of training is required, since the intention is to get bushy plants, but with the rapid and strong growth of most cultivars, it is easy to train them into a variety of shapes. Species fuchsias are the exception to this rule; most of them must be allowed to grow naturally.

SHAPES TO CHOOSE FROM

The natural desire of most fuchsias is to grow straight up along the central stem. If left to its own devices, this would produce a messy and unwieldy plant. The growth of a fuchsia, however, is easily manipulated; all that is needed to encourage bushiness, for example, is to remove the growing tip from the central stem, which will promote growth of sideshoots from the leaf axils.

This is called pinching. If even bushier plants are required, pinch the growing tips of each of the sideshoots as well (*see p.46*).

Standards (*see p.47*), espaliers (*see facing page*), columns, and pyramids are all relatively simple to train, but they need dedication, patience, and care, since it takes at least two years to achieve the shape required. In frost-prone climates, therefore,

RECOMMENDED SHAPES
Since fuchsias have a strong and vigorous tendency to grow straight up, most cultivars can be manipulated to grow into any of the shapes shown here. Always start with a strong, upright-growing cultivar. From left to right is 'Mieke Meursing' trained as a bush, 'Celia Smedley' as a standard, 'Display' as an espalier, 'Flirtation Waltz' as a pyramid, and 'Mrs Lovell Swisher' as a column.

Top growth is shaped in second year

Bare stem requires patient training

Bushy growth is promoted by regular pinching

BUSH

STANDARD

winter protection in heated accommodation will be necessary (*see p.39*).

Miniature versions of these structures can be achieved more quickly, and they are normally grown in smaller containers to achieve a balanced look between pot and plant. Since fuchsias rapidly become woody when grown in small pots, they also make good bonsai plants. Select a cultivar with small flowers and foliage, such as 'Postiljon'. Promote dense, bushy growth by continually pruning back during the first growing season; do the actual shaping during the second and third years.

Many fuchsias with thin, wiry growth (the Encliandra group in particular) can be used for topiary work. Trained around wire structures, they will quickly fill the desired shape and will produce a very pleasing effect with their flowers and foliage.

CREATING AN ESPALIER

An espalier is a plant trained with a vertical central stem and several tiers of branches growing horizontally on either side in a single plane. Fruit trees are commonly trained into espaliers, but the decorative, formal symmetry works just as well for fuchsias.

1 Take a strong, upright-growing bush fuchsia, and allow the sideshoots to develop.

2 Pinch out alternate sets of sideshoots, so that all of them grow along the same plane.

3 Train the sideshoots along a supporting frame so that they grow horizontally.

4 Pinch out the tip of the central stem once the structure has reached its desired height. Do the same with the sideshoots when they are sufficiently long; this also encourages the structure to fill out.

5 For a triangular espalier, like the one shown below, let the sideshoots at the bottom of the structure grow longer than the ones above.

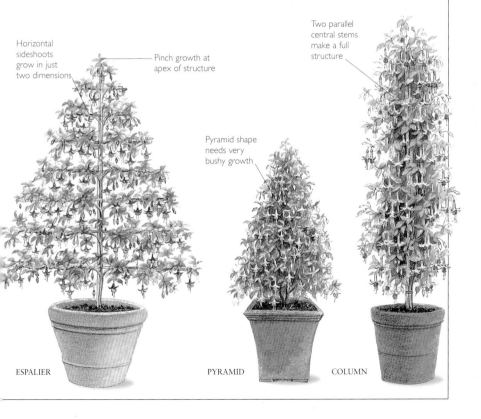

Horizontal sideshoots grow in just two dimensions

Pinch growth at apex of structure

Two parallel central stems make a full structure

Pyramid shape needs very bushy growth

ESPALIER

PYRAMID

COLUMN

PINCH PRUNING FOR BUSH FUCHSIAS

Fuchsias that will be grown as bushes in pots, in hanging containers, or in the border all require the same type of training. The object is to create a well-branched plant, and the more branches a fuchsia has, the more flowers it will give.

To encourage the growth of sideshoots, the upward growth must be stopped, which is simply achieved by removing the growing tip from the main shoot. The energy of the plant will now be directed toward the buds, which are in each of the leaf axils on the stem. These will grow and within about four weeks, each will have developed two or three sets of leaves with their own growing tips. The process can be repeated two or three times until the plant is sufficiently bushy; then allow it to mature and flower (*see below*). Bear in mind, however, that each pinching of the branches delays flowering.

As the plant matures, turn it regularly so that each side gets a fair share of light, which ensures even flowering. The use of a reflector box (a box lined with aluminium foil) is very convenient in the first days of spring if cuttings are kept on a windowsill.

1 **Remove the** growing tip of the main stem to promote growth of sideshoots.

2 **After a few weeks,** pinch out the growing tips of each new sideshoot to encourage more branching.

3 **Let the plant** mature after a final pinching out of the latest sideshoots. The first flowers should appear in about 8–10 weeks.

A FAN-TRAINED BUSH FUCHSIA
The growth of this bush fuchsia has been forced to branch out at an early age. Each branch has then been trained along a supporting cane to give its final shape.

TRAINING FUCHSIAS AS STANDARDS

To get a head start on training a standard, encourage autumn cuttings to grow steadily through winter by keeping them warm and well lit (*see p.39*). The greater part of the height will be achieved prior to rapid growth in spring. Choice of cultivar is not all that important, since any fuchsia can be trained as a standard, but select only cuttings that are growing straight up. A boost with balanced fertilizer ensures strong growth.

1 **Pinch out** any sideshoots as they appear in the leaf axils. Insert a stake and tie in the stem.

2 **Keep removing** sideshoots to make a tall, straight stem, but do not remove the stem leaves.

3 **When the stem** is 3 leaf sets taller than required, pinch out the tip. Repot and restake if necessary.

4 **Pinch out** the tips of the sideshoots at the top of the stem. Repeat until a round head is formed.

SUITABLE PLANTS

'Annabel' Makes a weeping standard with pale flowers.
'Barbara' Strong bushy growth; pale pink flowers.
'Border Queen' Great bush with two-toned flowers.
'Celia Smedley' Distinctive, easy-to-train bush.
'Checkerboard' Excellent bush; red and white flowers.
'Hawkshead' Bush; one of the best white-flowered types.
'La Campanella' Makes a floriferous weeping standard.
'Liebriez' Bush; good as a mini standard.
'Lindisfarne' Bush; good as a mini standard.
'Nellie Nuttall' Bush; easily trained into most shapes.
'Phyllis' Easy-to-train bush.
'Postiljon' Weeping standard.
'Thalia' A Triphylla bush with orange-scarlet flowers.

A FINISHED STANDARD
As soon as the head has bushed out, remove all the leaves on the tall stem. Keep the plant anchored to its stake, as this will give the stem greater strength.

PESTS AND DISEASES

L IKE SO MANY OTHER PLANTS, fuchsias are troubled by certain pests and diseases, some of which will cause serious damage if they are left untreated. As always, the prevention is better than the cure, although the methods of treatment are usually quite straightforward. With careful management and regular inspection of your plants, you can prevent pests and diseases from gaining the upper hand.

DIAGNOSIS AND TREATMENT

APHIDS AND WHITEFLIES

Aphids are unmistakable pests found around growing tips, sucking the sap from young plants to leave the growth distorted and stunted. The foliage may become yellow and drop off, and a sticky honeydew remains, which looks unsightly, attracting ants and encouraging the growth of sooty mould. Whiteflies live on leaf undersides and appear in clouds when a heavily infested plant is disturbed. Spray with a strong jet of water, an insecticide, or a weak solution of washing-up liquid. *Encarsia formosa*, a biological control, is available for whitefly.

VINE WEEVIL LARVAE
If a potted fuchsia wilts without warning, remove the pot and examine the roots. It is possible that you will find grubs like these.

CAPSID BUGS

Typically found on hardy fuchsias outdoors, especially if they grow near trees. These are sap-sucking insects that cause many small holes in leaves, leaf distortion, and failure of flower buds. To treat, spray with insecticide.

TROUBLE WITH WHITEFLIES
Whiteflies are easy to see when present in large numbers, such as on these badly infested leaves.

FROGHOPPERS

These small insects can cause distortion if feeding at the shoot tips. The larvae produce a frothy white liquid (cuckoo spit) and hide within it. Wash them off with a strong jet of water, hand pick, or apply an insecticide.

GREY MOULD (*BOTRYTIS*)

Browning then blackening of young stems, with furry grey mould, are the first signs of this disease. It usually arises as a result of neglect: careless watering, bad handling, or poor air flow. Treatment with fungicide is effective, although good ventilation will prevent the disease from occurring.

RED SPIDER MITES

One of the worst fuchsia pests, these tiny yellow-green mites usually appear on greenhouse plants. Although they are barely visible to the naked eye, the symptoms are clear: bronzed leaves, fine webbing, and eventual defoliation. The mites spread quickly and are treated by regular and thorough spraying with water or an insecticide. *Phytoseiulus persimilis* is a biological control. Maintain humidity as a preventive measure.

RUST

The early symptoms of rust are brown spots on the upper surface of the leaves, with pale orange pustules below. They look similar to rust found on metal, so the disease is well named. Remove infected leaves and spray with a fungicide, but take care as fuchsias are sensitive to some sprays.

THRIPS

These tiny, slender insects suck sap and may be visible on flowers, particularly in hot weather when they proliferate. Mist plants regularly to increase humidity under glass when temperatures are high, or use an appropriate insecticide.

SOOTY MOULD
The honeydew deposited by aphids tends to be a breeding place for sooty mould fungus, which causes the leaves to discolour and die.

VINE WEEVIL

The larvae of this pest eat fuchsia roots, causing sudden wilting of the plant. The most effective controls are either using a special potting compost containing a slow-release pesticide, or watering plants in pots with a pathogenic nematode in late summer.

DIAGNOSIS CHECKLIST

SYMPTOM	CAUSE
Falling and yellowing of leaves	Aphids
Stunted growth	Aphids
Sooty deposits of honeydew	Aphids or whiteflies
Distorted tips	Aphids, capsid bugs, froghoppers, or whiteflies
Distortion and holes in leaves	Capsid bugs
Lack of flowers	Capsid bugs
Frothy white liquid on stems	Froghoppers
Furry grey mould	Grey mould
Stems and shoots turning brown and black, often accompanied by furry grey mould	Grey mould
Ants crawling all over plant	Honeydew deposited by aphids
Bronzing of foliage and leaf fall	Red spider mites
Fine webbing between leaves	Red spider mites
Orange spores on leaves	Rust
Silver spotting on foliage	Thrips
Silver spotting on flowers	Thrips
Plants collapsing	Vine weevil (larvae)
Notches in leaf margins	Vine weevil (adults)

SEASONAL CALENDAR

SPRING

• To encourage new top growth on tender fuchsias, prune back old branches so that there are two or three old leaf joints with young buds awaiting development (*see p.39*).

• Repot fuchsias to stimulate root growth (*see p.38*). Remove as much of the old compost as possible, trim off any old and gnarled roots, and replace the fuchsias into clean pots of a size that will comfortably take the new root ball (this is often the same size as the pots from which they were taken). Keep an eye open for vine weevil larvae (*see p.49*).

• Regularly spray the top branches with tepid water to soften the young buds and encourage new growth.

• Be alert for signs of pests and diseases, particularly aphids (*see pp.48–49*).

• Take small soft-tip cuttings when they become available. Have the shape of your new plants in mind when the cuttings are removed (*see pp.40–41*).

• Keep cuttings at about 16°C (61°F) in an enclosed propagator (*see pp.41 and 42*). Spray regularly any cuttings in an open propagator.

• When cuttings are well rooted, pot up each into its own 8cm (3in) container (*see p.43*).

• Start the training process (*see pp.44–47*). Select those cuttings you wish to use for bushes, baskets, or standards.

• As the new plants fill their pots, it will be necessary to pot them on into larger containers (*see p.43*).

• Begin to feed plants with a balanced fertilizer in late spring (*see p.36*).

• Visit garden centres or specialist fuchsia nurseries if you wish to supplement your collection with new cultivars.

• Consider trying some of the Species or Encliandra fuchsias.

• Keep plants in greenhouses shaded from strong sun and keep ventilators and doors open whenever possible (*see p.37*).

• Cut back old growth on hardy fuchsias, which have overwintered in the open garden, as soon as new strong growth appears from the root system (*see p.39*).

• Make up hanging containers using fuchsias of a single cultivar, or a mixed planting with other trailing plants (*see pp.32–35*). Grow them outside, but only when the weather is favourable – be ready to take them under cover if late frosts are forecast.

• Once all risk of frost has passed, fuchsias may be planted outside in the border, and hanging containers can be placed in their final outdoor positions.

SUMMER

• Continue to feed plants growing in containers with a balanced fertilizer (*see p.36*).

• In drought periods, regularly water the soil around your plants in order to maintain a moistness, as opposed to wetness. The use of water-retaining granules in hanging baskets or planters may be beneficial.

• Continue to pot on developing fuchsias so that their root systems are not restricted (*see p.43*).

• Continue to take cuttings (*see p.40*), but take care to keep them cool – about 16°C (61°F).

• The training process (pinching of growth tips) must stop in sufficient time for the plants to develop flower buds, taking about 8–10 weeks after the final pinch (*see pp.44–47*).

• Keep a very careful eye open for attacks by aphids (*see p.48*).

• If insecticides are needed, read labels carefully before use.

• Support strong upward-growing branches with canes, if necessary.

LOOK AFTER THE MAIN STEM
Encourage growth at the head of a standard by removing any shoots that develop from its bare stem during the growing season. Also ensure that the stake is securely in place, as the main stem can easily snap.

SEASONAL CALENDAR

TIME TO PLANT UP A HANGING BASKET
Even though baskets will not be displayed in their final positions until all risk of frost has passed, they benefit from a head start by planting up in late spring and early summer.

• Remove any spent flowers before they have the opportunity to develop into berries (*see p.36*). If berries are allowed to develop, then the continuity of flowering will be impaired.
• Regularly water and feed fuchsias growing in the open garden during dry periods, especially fuchsias in the hardy border that are in their first season (*see p.36*).
• Pay particular attention to the watering and feeding of tender fuchsias plunged outside in the border in their pots.

AUTUMN

• Continue to feed and water your fuchsias (*see p.36*).
• Remove any flowers past their best to encourage further development of flower buds (*see p.36*).
• Keep a careful eye on the weather forecast and be prepared to take under cover, or to protect, any plants that might be damaged by frost. Pay special attention to both hanging containers and standards.
• Give consideration to the overwintering of those fuchsias that you wish to keep for the next growing season (*see p.39*).
• Feed with a high-potash nutrient, such as tomato or rose fertilizer, to help the wood ripen prior to overwintering.
• Take cuttings from plants braving the winter outside as an insurance against possible losses (*see p.40*).
• Outside, leave hardy fuchsias unpruned, but add a mulch of some insulating material, such as bark chippings or straw, around the crowns for winter protection (*see p.39*).

WINTER

• Ensure those tender fuchsias that are to be kept through the winter are in a frost-free position. Do not let the root system dry out completely (*see p.39*).
• All standard fuchsias should be brought indoors for winter protection. Protect them in three places: the root system (cover the pots with any insulating material), the stem (enclose in pipe-lagging tube), and the head (trim back slightly and cover with a good wrapping of horticultural fleece).
• Outdoors, check on frost-hardy fuchsias regularly, and replace any mulch that has been scratched away by birds or other animals.
• Fuchsias that are ticking over in a heated greenhouse will require a temperature in the region of 5–7°C (41–45°F) to keep the leaves from dropping.
• For fuchsias under cover, water should be carefully applied, and only if necessary.
• On mild days, allow air to circulate through the greenhouse by opening vents and doors.
• Cuttings taken in autumn can be potted on once they are rooted (*see p.43*), but keep them warm and as close to the light as possible.

SOFT-TIP CUTTINGS
This is the easiest and quickest way to propagate fuchsias (see p.40). Cuttings can be taken almost all year round, although the best time is autumn or spring. Take several cuttings to insure against failure.

A GALLERY OF FUCHSIAS

THE FUCHSIAS DESCRIBED HERE are grouped into three divisions: the gallery begins with Species fuchsias, followed by Triphyllas, and the final section is an A–Z of popular cultivars. Those fuchsias marked with the symbol ❋ are tolerant of frost; if this symbol is absent and you live in a climate with cold winters, assume that the plant will not survive outdoors. The symbol ♀ denotes the RHS Award of Garden Merit, which indicates outstanding garden value. Where a fuchsia is particularly suited to a certain use, this is stated; if not, then it is versatile.

SPECIES FUCHSIAS

THESE ARE THE FUCHSIAS FOUND IN THE WILD and the ancestors of all the modern cultivated varieties. Over one hundred Species fuchsias have been identified, and both plants and individual flowers vary considerably in size, but the majority are distinguished by long, colourful tubes with trumpet-shaped flowers. Hummingbirds usually pollinate wild fuchsias, attracted by the bright colours and rich nectar, yet the flowers have virtually no scent. Although Species fuchsias are often difficult to grow, requiring a lot of soil space for the roots to develop fully, they can be among the most rewarding of all fuchsias.

F. arborescens
Large clusters of small lilac blooms give this large shrub its name, "the lilac fuchsia".

F. x bacillaris
An Encliandra fuchsia, with a bushy habit and distinctive small leaves and flowers.

F. cordifolia
A bushy fuchsia with slender, multi-coloured flowers against a background of broad leaves.

◀ 'AUNTIE JINKS' *A very free-flowering, trailing cultivar, excellent for hanging containers.*

F. boliviana
This unusual fuchsia can be
encouraged to climb. Allow
the roots to spread out fully.

F. boliviana var. **alba** ♀
A climber, like *F. boliviana*,
but with white-tubed flowers.
Allow plenty of root space.

F. corymbiflora var. **alba**
A bush fuchsia with very
narrow flowers. The tubes
and sepals are pinkish white.

F. fulgens ♀
A very vigorous, upright,
and bushy fuchsia. One of
the easiest Species to grow.

F. hatsbachii
A good traditional-style
fuchsia, like *F. magellanica*.
The stems are wiry.

'Rubra Grandiflora'
This cultivar of *F. fulgens*
has upright and bushy growth.
It needs a large container.

F. hemsleyana
An upright-growing shrub,
with tiny flowers, growing
up to 75cm (30in) in the wild.

'Hinnerike'
A Species hybrid with delicate
flowers. Pinch out new growth
to encourage a bushy shape.

'Loxensis' ♀
A rampant, upright, and bushy
Species hybrid. It forms a
good shape without training.

F. lycioides
Trailing, bushy growth with
fleshy leaves and small
flowers. Drought resistant.

F. magellanica var. *gracilis* ✼
Upright and vigorous bush
with strong, wiry stems. The
flowers are relatively small.

F. procumbens ✼
Easy to grow with attractive,
long creeping stems, and small,
upward-looking flowers.

F. paniculata
A good Species fuchsia for the
beginner, strong-growing and
easy to train. Bushy growth.

F. magellanica ✼
There are many cultivars of this
Species, like *F. magellanica* var.
molinae 'Enstone' (*see p.69*).

F. simplicicaulis
An upright and quite vigorous
bush that bears long-tubed,
crimson flowers.

MORE SPECIES

F. excorticata Reaches a
large size with care. Small,
purplish flowers and
unusual blue pollen.
F. glazioviana Strong and
easy to grow. The small
flowers have red sepals
and violet petals.
F. magellanica 'Versicolor'
♀ ✼ Upright with grey-green
leaves, rose-tinted at first.
Red and purple blooms.
F. venusta Strong, spreading
bush. Overwinter for best
results. Red blooms.

TRIPHYLLA FUCHSIAS

'Billy Green' ♀
A superb bush fuchsia with
a profusion of flowers.

THIS EXCELLENT GROUP OF PLANTS is well worth growing. The flowers are distinguished by their particularly long tubes and trumpet-shaped sepals and petals, and the blooms are generally held in large bunches at the ends of branches. The leaves are usually dark green in colour, often with an attractive purple sheen underneath. Triphylla fuchsias are susceptible to frost, so they are best grown as summer plants, but with patience they may be trained as beautiful standards to provide added height and colour to summer plantings.

'Coralle' ♀
An upright and vigorous
bush, with tapering flowers
about 6cm (2½in) long.

'Edwin J. Goulding'
An excellent border addition,
producing a profusion of red
flowers throughout summer.

'Mary' ♀
This eye-catching fuchsia has
bright crimson flowers, and
leaves with purple undersides.

'Peter Crooks'
A trailing bush suitable for
hanging baskets. The flowers
are produced in bunches.

'Stella Ann'
A vigorous, upright fuchsia.
The foliage is olive-green with
purple midribs, red beneath.

'Thalia' ♀
A strong grower, but early
training is recommended
for a good shape.

POPULAR CULTIVARS

'André Le Nostre'
Introduced in 1909, this
strong bush is still popular.

WITH OVER TEN THOUSAND CULTIVARS to choose from, there must be a fuchsia for everyone, from classic single flowers to large and exuberant doubles, from purest white to red, pink, and purple. All are easy to grow and propagate, and they are ideal for summer colour, whether grown in pots, on patios, in hanging containers, or planted permanently in the open garden. The hardy cultivars, if planted deeply, will survive most winters in frosty areas, to provide a wealth of flowers and neat foliage through summer and into autumn.

'Annabel' ♀
A very versatile, trailing bush,
adaptable for bushes, baskets,
or standards. Easily trained.

'Andrew Hadfield'
This very free-flowering bush
is good in a pot. The petals
flare as the flower matures.

'Atlantic Star'
The compact growth of this
single-flowered bush makes it
a good choice for containers.

'Autumnale'
An attractive trailing fuchsia
for a hanging basket. Grown
for its colourful young leaves.

'Aunt Juliana'
A trailing fuchsia good for
a hanging basket. It needs
support grown as a bush.

'Baby Pink'
A strong-growing double
fuchsia that makes an
excellent trailing plant.

'Ballet Girl'
A vigorous, bushy fuchsia
that makes a good standard.
It has fairly large blooms.

'Barbara'
A good bush fuchsia with
strong growth. Will also
train well as a standard.

'Bashful' ❋
With its profusion of small
flowers, this bush is ideal for
long-lasting outdoor display.

'Beacon Rosa'
Medium-sized blooms on
a strong, upright fuchsia.
The petals are lightly veined.

'Bicentennial'
A good trailer for a basket,
it will also train as an
impressive weeping standard.

'Bella Rosella'
This trailing fuchsia bears
very large, attractive double
blooms with magenta petals.

'Blush of Dawn'
A highly recommended trailer
with large and long-lasting,
fully double flowers.

'Carmel Blue'
A particularly fine blue and
white bush cultivar that
produces flowers freely.

'Cascade'
A superb cultivar for basket
display, producing a tumble
of flowers. Serrated foliage.

'Celebration'
A trailer with marbled petals and yellow-edged leaves. Suitable for a hanging basket.

'Celia Smedley' ♀
An excellent, very vigorous bush with vivid flowers. Also good as a standard.

'Checkerboard' ♀
This bush gives a succession of blooms through summer. An excellent beginner's cultivar.

'Dancing Flame'
A striking, double-flowered trailing cultivar. The large leaves have serrated edges.

'Deep Purple'
Vigorous and spreading, this double-flowered plant is good for a large hanging container.

'Dorothy'
Fairly hardy, this cultivar can be grown as a hedge in very mild areas.

'Dusky Beauty'
This cultivar bears a
profusion of small flowers
on bushy, upright growth.

'Duchess of Albany'
A free-flowering, strong-
growing bush, suitable for
training as a standard.

'Eternal Flame'
The semi-double flowers
stand out attractively against
the dark foliage of this bush.

'Fiona'
This strong and spreading
trailer is excellent in a hanging
basket. Finely serrated leaves.

'Frank Unsworth'
The superb flowers contrast
well with the small dark
leaves of this trailing fuchsia.

'Garden News' ♈ ❋
A hardy bush for the garden border, with ruffled flowers borne on sturdy branches.

'Frosted Flame'
The long, barrel-shaped flowers make this trailing fuchsia ideal for a basket.

'Genii' ♈ ❋
An upright bush with pretty foliage and stems that redden when grown in full sun.

'Glowing Embers'
Grown as either a bush or a trailer, this fuchsia is very free flowering with large blooms.

'Golden Marinka' ♈
The variegated foliage is best in full sun. An early-flowering trailer for a hanging basket.

'Grace Darling'
Bell-shaped blooms are
freely produced on this
bush with serrated leaves.

'Gretna Chase'
A free-flowering bush fuchsia,
with blooms of rose-pink and
white, and mid-green foliage.

'Gruss aus dem Bodethal'
This easy-to-grow bush
is famous for its striking,
very deeply coloured petals.

'Gwen Dodge'
A bush fuchsia that is very
free flowering. The blooms
are flared and look upward.

'Happy Wedding Day'
When open fully, this bush
bears very large, rounded
blooms. Needs support.

'Haute Cuisine'
Grown as a bush or trailer, this fuchsia bears large, deeply coloured double blooms.

'Harry Gray'
Excellent in hanging baskets, this trailer produces double blooms on short growth.

'Hermiena'
A self-branching trailer that flowers in profusion. Good for hanging baskets.

'Heidi Weiss'
An upright, self-branching bush with fully double blooms. The petals have scarlet veining.

'Hidcote Beauty'
A trailing bush with strong growth that is well suited to a container.

'Jack Shahan' ♀
This trailer flowers over a
long season. Pinch the stems
to maintain a good shape.

'Jim Coleman'
A strong, upright fuchsia
with semi-upright, bell-shaped
flowers produced freely.

'Jomam'
The slightly flared, bell-shaped
flowers of this bushy fuchsia
are borne in profusion.

'Joy Patmore' ♀
A distinctively coloured
fuchsia with green-tipped
sepals. Easily cultivated.

'Katrina Thompsen'
This is a superb, very
free-flowering bush. The
blooms are medium sized.

'Kegworth Carnival'
A good cultivar for a hanging basket. With support, it will grow as a bush.

'Komeet'
The petals on this reliable, upright bush change to red-lilac as they mature.

'La Campanella' ♀
A fine choice for a hanging basket, this trailing fuchsia develops rapidly once settled.

'Lady in Grey'
This double-flowered cultivar needs full sun. It is more difficult to grow than most.

'Lady Thumb' ♀ ✽
Small foliage and flowers on a small plant – no more than 30cm (12in) tall and wide.

'Land van Beveren'
A trailing fuchsia with waxy
white sepals that open to
reveal carmine-red petals.

'Lena' ♀ ✳
A highly versatile fuchsia
that can be grown in a pot
and trained into shapes.

'Leonora' ♀
This bush fuchsia bears many
soft pink flowers. The sepals
are tipped with green.

'Little Ouse'
A large-flowered cultivar
that may grow rapidly in
a single season.

'Loeky'
This fuchsia with delightful
flowers is suitable for training
as a small standard.

'Love's Reward'
A superb fuchsia that
gives great quantities of
flowers through the season.

'Lye's Unique'
A very popular, free-flowering cultivar with distinctive white and salmon-orange flowers.

F. magellanica var. *molinae* 'Enstone' ✻
This bush fuchsia is valued for its green and gold foliage. The flowers are red and purple.

'Machu Picchu'
Regularly pinch the shoot tips of this free-flowering fuchsia for a good shape.

'Major Heaphy'
Keep the soil moist around this free-flowering, upright bush or the flowers will drop.

'Margaret Brown' ♀ ✻
An excellent upright bush that flowers freely. Does well in the open garden.

'Margaret Pilkington'
The violet petals of this fairly strong, upright bush mature to soft purple.

'Marinka' ♀
A vigorous and very free-
flowering bush that makes a
superb hanging basket display.

'Micky Goult'
This fuchsia bears a profusion
of compact flowers. It is
useful in summer bedding.

'Mieke Meursing'
An upright bush with red-
veined flowers. Cold draughts
will mark the foliage.

'Mission Bells'
Good for summer bedding,
this is an upright, self-branching
bush with serrated foliage.

'Minirose'
Ideal for smaller standards,
this cultivar produces almost
square-shaped flowers.

'More Applause'
A trailer with large, fully
double flowers framed
by backward-curving sepals.

'Mrs Lovell Swisher'
Small flowers are produced
in great quantity on this
vigorous, upright bush.

'Moonbeam'
An upright, self-branching
cultivar with double blooms.
It may need support.

'Mrs Popple' ♀ ❋
A bushy cultivar with vivid
blooms among slender and
serrated leaves.

'Nellie Nuttall' ♀
This bush produces many
small blooms through its
long growing season.

'Orange Crush'
Striking salmon-orange
blooms are borne on this
free-flowering bush.

'Other Fellow'
Grown for its dainty, small
flowers, this is an upright,
self-branching bush.

'Paula Jane' ♀
A free-flowering upright
bush. The deep purple petals
mature to ruby red.

'Pink Bon Accorde'
An upright bush with small
to medium flowers, borne
slightly away from the foliage.

'Preston Guild'
This fuchsia bears plenty of
compact flowers. The sepals
flush pink when grown outside.

'Postiljon'
Vigorous and self-branching,
this is a good hanging basket
fuchsia with small flowers.

'President'
A fairly vigorous bush with
loosely formed, medium-
sized blooms.

'President Wilf Sharp'
A bush fuchsia that freely
bears medium-sized, double
blooms in shades of pink.

'Quasar'
The naturally trailing habit of this cultivar makes it useful for hanging containers.

'Rambling Rose'
A bushy, trailing plant for a hanging basket. Pinch out new shoots regularly.

'Queen's Park'
An upright bush, valued for its profusion of traditionally coloured flowers.

'Ridestar'
The flowers of this upright and bushy cultivar show a subtle combination of colours.

'Rose Lace' ❋
Large, full blooms are borne freely on this upright bush with arching stems.

'Rose of Denmark'
An old cultivar, with green-tipped sepals on rather loose blooms. A bush or trailer.

'Rosy Frills'
A good hanging basket cultivar with a very free-flowering, trailing habit.

'Royal Velvet' ♀
This vigorous bush has striking, richly coloured double flowers.

'Rufus' ✳
A self-branching bush that produces flowers freely throughout the season.

'San Diego'
A good trailer for a hanging basket, with pinkish white sepals and rose-red petals.

'Santa Cruz'
A very sturdy bush cultivar
with crimson blooms and
bronzed, serrated foliage.

'Sealand Prince'
An upright bush bearing
many medium-sized flowers
with narrow, upturned sepals.

'Sensation'
This trailer freely bears
huge flowers, which measure
over 13cm (5in) across.

'Snowcap' ♀
This upright, self-branching
cultivar flowers profusely.
Train growth early to shape.

'So Big'
This pretty trailing fuchsia
for a hanging basket bears
double blooms.

'Swingtime' ♀
A very vigorous trailer with
fluffy, fully double flowers.
An excellent basket fuchsia.

'Tom Thumb' ♀ ✳
Small flowers and leaves on
an upright, self-branching,
free-flowering bush fuchsia.

'Tom West'
A bush grown for its variegated
foliage, which is encouraged by
regular pinching of the shoot tips.

'Walsingham'
This cultivar freely produces
semi-double blooms. The
petals have crimped edges.

'Waveney Gem'
A free-flowering trailer
that will achieve an upright
shape if supported.

'Wedding Bells'
An almost pure white fuchsia.
The sepals are faintly pink
when mature. Bushy growth.

'Winston Churchill' ♀
An excellent, self-branching, bushy cultivar, producing compact blooms in quantity.

'Yuletide'
A very showy bush cultivar. Very free flowering, with vigorous, upright branches.

MORE CHOICES

'Ann Howard Tripp' Very free-flowering bush; pink and white semi-double blooms.

'Bealings' Bush; bright violet petals that mature to rose-pink, and white sepals.

'Bon Accorde' Bush good as a standard; white tubes and sepals, pale purple petals.

'Centerpiece' Bush or trailer; fairly large, red and lavender semi-double blooms.

'Charming' ✳ Splendid bush; yellowish green leaves complement red blooms.

'Crackerjack' Trailing habit; pink-flushed white blooms, mauve-white at petal bases.

'Dulcie Elizabeth' Bush; double flowers with pink sepals and rose-pink petals.

'Gillian Althea' Bush; double flowers with pink sepals, and unusual, light blue petals touched with orange.

'Hawkshead' ✳ Tall, strong bush; brilliant white flowers.

'Lakeland Princess' Upright and strong bush; red tubes, white sepals flushed with red, violet petals.

'Mayblossom' Trailing habit; small, white and rose-pink double flowers.

'Natasha Sinton' Trailer; pink and magenta double blooms.

'Olive Moon' Bush; semi-double blooms of pale pink and pale magenta.

'Rainbow' Strong, spreading trailer; red, dark pink, and violet double flowers with orange-red outer petals.

'Rosebud' Bushy habit, but needing support; white and rose-orange double blooms.

'Salmon Cascade' Trailer; pale pink sepals around deep orange-red petals.

'Son of Thumb' ✳ ♀ Superb low bush for a windowbox; cerise and lilac blooms.

'Wilson's Pearls' Trailer with red and white, semi-double blooms.

INDEX

ACKNOWLEDGMENTS

Picture research Cathie Arrington
Special photography Peter Anderson
Illustrations Gill Tomblin
Index Liz Granger

Dorling Kindersley would like to thank:
All staff at the RHS, in particular Susanne
Mitchell, Karen Wilson, and Barbara Haynes
at Vincent Square; Fiona Wild for editorial
assistance.

Photography
The publisher would also like to thank the
following for their kind permission to
reproduce their photographs:
(key: t=top, c=centre, b=below, l=left, r=right)

George Bartlett: 53br, 54tl, 54bl, 54br, 55tl,
55tr, 55cr, 55bl, 55bc, 55br, 56tr, 56bl, 56bc,
57c, 57bl, 57bc, 58tl, 58br, 59tr, 59cr, 59bc,
59br, 60cl, 60bl, 60br, 61cl, 61bl, 62cr, 62br,
63bl, 64tr, 65tr, 65cr, 65bl, 66br, 68tl, 68cl,
68bl, 69tr, 69bl, 69br, 70tr, 70br, 71bc, 72tl,
73tl, 73cl, 73br, 76cr, 76br, 77t
Garden Matters: 8br

Garden Picture Library: Lynn Brotchie 37b;
Chris Burrows 13bc, 15c; Eric Crichton 5bl,
14; Ron Evans 4br, 20l; John Glover 18, 19t;
Sunniva Harte 8t, 9, 52; Lamontagne 25t;
Marie O'Hara 23b; Howard Rice 2; J.S. Sira
8bl; Didier Willery 19b
John Glover: back cover tr and c, 13cr, 13bl,
20r, 21t
Harpur Garden Library: 16c, 21b
Andrew Lawson: 13c, 13br, 23t, 24b, 26
S&O Matthews Photography: 7, 17, 24t
Clive Nichols Garden Pictures: 6, 10bc,
12cr; Lower House Farm, Gwent 16b; Old
Rectory, Berkshire 25b
Harry Smith Collection: front cover r, 10bl,
10r, 11t, 11bl, 11br, 12bl, 12bc, 12br, 13cl,
15t, 70bl

The Royal Horticultural Society
To learn more about the work of the
Society, visit the RHS on the internet at
www.rhs.org.uk. Information includes news
of events around the country, a horticultural
database, international plant registers, results
of plant trials, and membership details.